Description:

_____

_____

_____

_____

_____

_____

_____

_____

_____

_____

_____

_____

Sky Placement:

Time:

Weather:

Lunar Phase:

Longitude:

Latitude:

Objects Sited:

_____

_____

_____

Equipment Used:

_____

MW00940168

1

Additional Notes:

_____

_____

_____

_____

_____

_____

_____

_____

_____

_____

_____

_____

_____

Sketches & Photos:

Description:

Date: ____/____/____

_____
_____
_____
_____
_____
_____
_____
_____
_____
_____
_____
_____
_____
_____
_____

Place:
_____

_____

Time:
_____

Weather:
_____

Lunar Phase:
_____

Longitude:
_____

Latitude:
_____

Objects Sited:
_____

_____

_____

_____

Equipment Used:
_____

Sky Placement:

Additional Notes:

_____

_____

_____

_____

_____

_____

_____

_____

_____

_____

_____

Sketches & Photos:

Description:

Date: ____/____/____

Place:

Time:

Weather:

Lunar Phase:

Longitude:

Latitude:

Objects Sited:

Equipment Used:

Sky Placement:

5

Additional Notes:

Date: ____/____/____

Sketches & Photos:

Description:

Date: ____/____/____

_____

_____

_____

_____

_____

_____

_____

_____

_____

_____

_____

_____

Sky Placement:

Place:

_____

_____

Time:

_____

Weather:

_____

Lunar Phase:

_____

Longitude:

_____

Latitude:

_____

Objects Sited:

_____

_____

_____

_____

Equipment Used:

_____

7

Additional Notes:

Date: ____/____/____

_____
_____
_____
_____
_____
_____
_____
_____
_____
_____
_____
_____
_____

Sketches & Photos:

Description:

Date: ___/___/___

Place:

Time:

Weather:

Lunar Phase:

Longitude:

Latitude:

Sky Placement:

Objects Sited:

Equipment Used:

Additional Notes:

_____

_____

_____

_____

_____

_____

_____

_____

_____

_____

_____

_____

Sketches & Photos:

Description:

Date: ____/____/____

_____

_____

_____

_____

_____

_____

_____

_____

_____

_____

_____

_____

Place:

_____

_____

Time:

_____

Weather:

_____

Lunar Phase:

_____

Longitude:

_____

Latitude:

_____

Objects Sited:

_____

_____

_____

_____

Equipment Used:

_____

Sky Placement:

Additional Notes:

Date: _____/_____/_____

_____

_____

_____

_____

_____

_____

_____

_____

_____

_____

_____

_____

Sketches & Photos:

Description:

Date: ____/____/____

_____

_____

_____

_____

_____

_____

_____

_____

_____

_____

_____

Sky Placement:

Place:

_____

_____

Time:

_____

Weather:

_____

Lunar Phase:

_____

Longitude:

_____

Latitude:

_____

Objects Sited:

_____

_____

_____

Equipment Used:

_____

13

Additional Notes:

_____
_____
_____
_____
_____
_____
_____
_____
_____
_____
_____
_____

Sketches & Photos:

Description:

Date: ____/____/____

_____

_____

_____

_____

_____

_____

_____

_____

_____

_____

_____

Sky Placement:

Place:

_____

_____

Time:

_____

Weather:

_____

Lunar Phase:

_____

Longitude:

_____

Latitude:

_____

Objects Sited:

_____

_____

_____

_____

Equipment Used:

_____

Additional Notes:

Date: ____/____/____

Sketches & Photos:

Description:

Date: ____/____/____

_____
_____
_____
_____
_____
_____
_____
_____
_____
_____
_____
_____

Place:

_____

_____

Time:

_____

Weather:

_____

Lunar Phase:

_____

Longitude:

_____

Latitude:

_____

Objects Sited:

_____

_____

_____

_____

Equipment Used:

_____

Sky Placement:

Additional Notes:

Sketches & Photos:

Description:

Date: ___/___/____

Place:

Time:

Weather:

Lunar Phase:

Longitude:

Latitude:

Objects Sited:

Equipment Used:

Sky Placement:

19

Additional Notes:

Date: ____/____/____

Sketches & Photos:

Description:

Date: ____/____/____

_____

_____

_____

_____

_____

_____

_____

_____

_____

_____

_____

_____

Sky Placement:

Place:

_____

_____

Time:

_____

Weather:

_____

Lunar Phase:

_____

Longitude:

_____

Latitude:

_____

Objects Sited:

_____

_____

_____

_____

Equipment Used:

_____

Additional Notes:

Sketches & Photos:

Description:

Date: ____/____/____

_____

_____

_____

_____

_____

_____

_____

_____

_____

_____

_____

_____

Sky Placement:

Place:

_____

_____

Time:

_____

Weather:

_____

Lunar Phase:

_____

Longitude:

_____

Latitude:

_____

Objects Sited:

_____

_____

_____

_____

Equipment Used:

_____

23

Additional Notes:

Date: _____/_____/_____

_____

_____

_____

_____

_____

_____

_____

_____

_____

_____

_____

Sketches & Photos:

Description:

Date: ____/____/____

Place:
_____
_____

Time:
_____

Weather:
_____

Lunar Phase:
_____

Longitude:
_____

Latitude:
_____

Objects Sited:
_____
_____
_____
_____

Sky Placement:

Equipment Used:
_____

25

Additional Notes:

Date: ____ / ____ / ____

_____

_____

_____

_____

_____

_____

_____

_____

_____

_____

_____

_____

Sketches & Photos:

Description:

Date: ____/____/____

_____

_____

_____

_____

_____

_____

_____

_____

_____

_____

_____

_____

Place:

_____

_____

Time:

_____

Weather:

_____

Lunar Phase:

_____

Longitude:

_____

Latitude:

_____

Objects Sited:

_____

_____

_____

_____

Equipment Used:

_____

Sky Placement:

Additional Notes:

Date: _____/_____/_____

Sketches & Photos:

Description:

Date: _____/_____/_____

_____

_____

_____

_____

_____

_____

_____

_____

_____

_____

_____

_____

_____

Place:

_____

_____

Time:

_____

Weather:

_____

Lunar Phase:

_____

Longitude:

_____

Latitude:

_____

Objects Sited:

_____

_____

_____

_____

Equipment Used:

_____

Sky Placement:

Additional Notes:

_____

_____

_____

_____

_____

_____

_____

_____

_____

_____

_____

_____

Sketches & Photos:

Description:

Date: ____/____/____

_____

_____

_____

_____

_____

_____

_____

_____

_____

_____

_____

_____

Sky Placement:

Place:

_____

_____

Time:

_____

Weather:

_____

Lunar Phase:

_____

Longitude:

_____

Latitude:

_____

Objects Sited:

_____

_____

_____

_____

Equipment Used:

_____

Additional Notes:

_____

_____

_____

_____

_____

_____

_____

_____

_____

_____

_____

_____

_____

Sketches & Photos:

Description:

Date: ___/___/___

_____
_____
_____
_____
_____
_____
_____
_____
_____
_____
_____
_____
_____

Sky Placement:

Place:

_____

_____

Time:

_____

Weather:

_____

Lunar Phase:

_____

Longitude:

_____

Latitude:

_____

Objects Sited:

_____

_____

_____

_____

Equipment Used:

_____

33

Additional Notes:

_____
_____
_____
_____
_____
_____
_____
_____
_____
_____
_____
_____

Sketches & Photos:

Description: Date: ___/___/___

_____   Place:

_____   _____

_____   _____

_____   Time:

_____   _____

_____   Weather:

_____   _____

_____   Lunar Phase:

_____   _____

_____   Longitude:

_____   _____

Sky Placement: Latitude:

                                          _____

                                          Objects Sited:

                                          _____

                                          _____

                                          _____

                                          _____

                                          Equipment Used:

                                          _____

Additional Notes:

_____

_____

_____

_____

_____

_____

_____

_____

_____

_____

_____

_____

Sketches & Photos:

Description:

Date: ____/____/____

_____

_____

_____

_____

_____

_____

_____

_____

_____

_____

_____

_____

_____

Sky Placement:

Place:

_____

_____

Time:

_____

Weather:

_____

Lunar Phase:

_____

Longitude:

_____

Latitude:

_____

Objects Sited:

_____

_____

_____

_____

Equipment Used:

_____

Additional Notes:

Date: ____/____/____

_____
_____
_____
_____
_____
_____
_____
_____
_____
_____
_____

Sketches & Photos:

Description:

Date: ____/____/____

_____
_____
_____
_____
_____
_____
_____
_____
_____
_____
_____
_____
_____
_____

Sky Placement:

Place:
_____
_____

Time:
_____

Weather:
_____

Lunar Phase:
_____

Longitude:
_____

Latitude:
_____

Objects Sited:
_____
_____
_____
_____

Equipment Used:
_____

39

Additional Notes:

Sketches & Photos:

Description:

Date: ____/____/____

_____

_____

_____

_____

_____

_____

_____

_____

_____

_____

_____

Place:

_____

_____

Time:

_____

Weather:

_____

Lunar Phase:

_____

Longitude:

_____

Latitude:

_____

Objects Sited:

_____

_____

_____

_____

Equipment Used:

_____

Sky Placement:

Additional Notes:

Date: _____/_____/_____

_____
_____
_____
_____
_____
_____
_____
_____
_____
_____
_____
_____
_____

Sketches & Photos:

Description:

Date: ____/____/____

_____

_____

_____

_____

_____

_____

_____

_____

_____

_____

_____

_____

_____

_____

_____

Sky Placement:

Place:

_____

_____

Time:

_____

Weather:

_____

Lunar Phase:

_____

Longitude:

_____

Latitude:

_____

Objects Sited:

_____

_____

_____

_____

Equipment Used:

_____

Additional Notes:

Date: _____ / _____ / _____

_____

_____

_____

_____

_____

_____

_____

_____

_____

_____

_____

_____

_____

Sketches & Photos:

Description:

Date: ____/____/____

_____

_____

_____

_____

_____

_____

_____

_____

_____

_____

_____

_____

Sky Placement:

Place:

_____

_____

Time:

_____

Weather:

_____

Lunar Phase:

_____

Longitude:

_____

Latitude:

_____

Objects Sited:

_____

_____

_____

_____

Equipment Used:

_____

Additional Notes:

Date: ____/____/____

_____

_____

_____

_____

_____

_____

_____

_____

_____

_____

_____

_____

_____

Sketches & Photos:

Description:

Date: ____/____/____

_____
_____
_____
_____
_____
_____
_____
_____
_____
_____
_____
_____

Sky Placement:

Place:
_____

_____

Time:
_____

Weather:
_____

Lunar Phase:
_____

Longitude:
_____

Latitude:
_____

Objects Sited:
_____
_____
_____

Equipment Used:
_____

Additional Notes:

_____

_____

_____

_____

_____

_____

_____

_____

_____

_____

_____

_____

Sketches & Photos:

Description:

Date: ____/____/____

_____

_____

_____

_____

_____

_____

_____

_____

_____

_____

_____

_____

Sky Placement:

Place:

_____

_____

Time:

_____

Weather:

_____

Lunar Phase:

_____

Longitude:

_____

Latitude:

_____

Objects Sited:

_____

_____

_____

_____

Equipment Used:

_____

Additional Notes:

_____
_____
_____
_____
_____
_____
_____
_____
_____
_____
_____
_____
_____

Sketches & Photos:

Description:

Date: ____/____/____

Place:
_____
_____

Time:
_____

Weather:
_____

Lunar Phase:
_____

Longitude:
_____

Latitude:
_____

Objects Sited:
_____
_____
_____
_____

Equipment Used:
_____

Sky Placement:

Additional Notes:

Sketches & Photos:

Description:

Date: ____/____/____

_____
_____
_____
_____
_____
_____
_____
_____
_____
_____
_____
_____
_____
_____

Place:

_____

_____

Time:

_____

Weather:

_____

Lunar Phase:

_____

Longitude:

_____

Latitude:

_____

Objects Sited:

_____

_____

_____

_____

Equipment Used:

_____

Sky Placement:

Additional Notes:

Date: _____ / _____ / _____

_____
_____
_____
_____
_____
_____
_____
_____
_____
_____
_____
_____

Sketches & Photos:

Description:

Date: ___/___/___

Place:

_____

_____

Time:

_____

Weather:

_____

Lunar Phase:

_____

Longitude:

_____

Latitude:

_____

Objects Sited:

_____

_____

_____

Sky Placement:

Equipment Used:

_____

55

Additional Notes:

Date: ____/____/____

_____
_____
_____
_____
_____
_____
_____
_____
_____
_____
_____
_____
_____

Sketches & Photos:

Description:

Date: ____/____/____

_____
_____
_____
_____
_____
_____
_____
_____
_____
_____
_____
_____
_____

Sky Placement:

Place:

_____

_____

Time:

_____

Weather:

_____

Lunar Phase:

_____

Longitude:

_____

Latitude:

_____

Objects Sited:

_____

_____

_____

Equipment Used:

_____

Additional Notes:

_____

_____

_____

_____

_____

_____

_____

_____

_____

_____

_____

_____

Sketches & Photos:

Description:

Place:

Time:

Weather:

Lunar Phase:

Longitude:

Sky Placement:

Latitude:

Objects Sited:

Equipment Used:

Additional Notes:

Date: ____/____/____

_____
_____
_____
_____
_____
_____
_____
_____
_____
_____
_____
_____
_____

Sketches & Photos:

Description:

_____

_____

_____

_____

_____

_____

_____

_____

_____

_____

_____

_____

Sky Placement:

Date: _____/_____/_____

Place:

_____

_____

Time:

_____

Weather:

_____

Lunar Phase:

_____

Longitude:

_____

Latitude:

_____

Objects Sited:

_____

_____

_____

_____

Equipment Used:

_____

61

Additional Notes: Date: ____/____/____

_____

_____

_____

_____

_____

_____

_____

_____

_____

_____

_____

_____

Sketches & Photos:

Description:

Date: ____/____/____

_____

_____

_____

_____

_____

_____

_____

_____

_____

_____

_____

Place:

_____

_____

Time:

_____

Weather:

_____

Lunar Phase:

_____

Longitude:

_____

Latitude:

_____

Sky Placement:

Objects Sited:

_____

_____

_____

_____

Equipment Used:

_____

Additional Notes:

Date: ____/____/____

Sketches & Photos:

Description:

Date: ____/____/____

_____

_____

_____

_____

_____

_____

_____

_____

_____

_____

_____

_____

Sky Placement:

Place:

_____

_____

Time:

_____

Weather:

_____

Lunar Phase:

_____

Longitude:

_____

Latitude:

_____

Objects Sited:

_____

_____

_____

_____

Equipment Used:

_____

Additional Notes: Date: ____/____/____

Sketches & Photos:

Description:

Date: ___/___/___

_____
_____
_____
_____
_____
_____
_____
_____
_____
_____
_____

Place:
_____
_____

Time:
_____

Weather:
_____

Lunar Phase:
_____

Longitude:
_____

Latitude:
_____

Objects Sited:
_____
_____
_____
_____

Equipment Used:
_____

Sky Placement:

67

Additional Notes:

Date: _____/_____/_____

Sketches & Photos:

Description:

Date: ____/____/____

_____

_____

_____

_____

_____

_____

_____

_____

_____

_____

_____

Sky Placement:

Place:

_____

_____

Time:

_____

Weather:

_____

Lunar Phase:

_____

Longitude:

_____

Latitude:

_____

Objects Sited:

_____

_____

_____

Equipment Used:

_____

Additional Notes:

_____

_____

_____

_____

_____

_____

_____

_____

_____

_____

_____

_____

Sketches & Photos:

Description:

Date: ___/___/___

_____

_____

_____

_____

_____

_____

_____

_____

_____

_____

_____

Sky Placement:

Place:

_____

_____

Time:

_____

Weather:

_____

Lunar Phase:

_____

Longitude:

_____

Latitude:

_____

Objects Sited:

_____

_____

_____

_____

Equipment Used:

_____

71

Additional Notes:

_____
_____
_____
_____
_____
_____
_____
_____
_____
_____
_____

Sketches & Photos:

Description:

_____

_____

_____

_____

_____

_____

_____

_____

_____

_____

_____

Sky Placement:

Place:

_____

_____

Time:

_____

Weather:

_____

Lunar Phase:

_____

Longitude:

_____

Latitude:

_____

Objects Sited:

_____

_____

_____

_____

Equipment Used:

_____

Additional Notes:

Sketches & Photos:

Description: Date: ___/___/___

_____   Place:
_____
_____   _____
_____
_____   _____
_____
_____   Time:
_____
_____   _____
_____
_____   Weather:
_____
_____   _____
_____
                                      Lunar Phase:

                                      _____

Sky Placement: Longitude:

                                      _____

                                      Latitude:

                                      _____

                                      Objects Sited:

                                      _____

                                      _____

                                      _____

                                      _____

                                      Equipment Used:

                                      _____

75

Additional Notes:

Sketches & Photos:

Description:

Date: ____/____/____

Place:
_____
_____

Time:
_____

Weather:
_____

Lunar Phase:
_____

Longitude:
_____

Latitude:
_____

Objects Sited:
_____
_____
_____
_____

Equipment Used:
_____

Sky Placement:

Additional Notes:

_____
_____
_____
_____
_____
_____
_____
_____
_____
_____
_____
_____

Sketches & Photos:

Description:

Date: ____/____/____

Place:

_____

_____

Time:

_____

Weather:

_____

Lunar Phase:

_____

Longitude:

_____

Latitude:

_____

Objects Sited:

_____

_____

_____

_____

Equipment Used:

_____

Sky Placement:

Additional Notes:

Date: ____/____/____

Sketches & Photos:

Description:

Date: ____/____/____

_____

_____

_____

_____

_____

_____

_____

_____

_____

_____

_____

_____

Sky Placement:

Place:

_____

_____

Time:

_____

Weather:

_____

Lunar Phase:

_____

Longitude:

_____

Latitude:

_____

Objects Sited:

_____

_____

_____

_____

Equipment Used:

_____

81

Additional Notes:

Date: ____/____/____

_____

Sketches & Photos:

Description:

Date: ___/___/___

Place:
_____
_____

Time:
_____

Weather:
_____

Lunar Phase:
_____

Longitude:
_____

Latitude:
_____

Objects Sited:
_____
_____
_____
_____

Sky Placement:

Equipment Used:
_____

Additional Notes: Date: ____/____/____

_____
_____
_____
_____
_____
_____
_____
_____
_____
_____
_____
_____

Sketches & Photos:

Description:

Date: ____/____/____

Place:

Time:

Weather:

Lunar Phase:

Longitude:

Latitude:

Sky Placement:

Objects Sited:

Equipment Used:

85

Additional Notes:

Sketches & Photos:

Description:

Date: ____/____/____

_____

_____

_____

_____

_____

_____

_____

_____

_____

_____

_____

_____

Sky Placement:

Place:

_____

_____

Time:

_____

Weather:

_____

Lunar Phase:

_____

Longitude:

_____

Latitude:

_____

Objects Sited:

_____

_____

_____

_____

Equipment Used:

_____

Additional Notes:

Date: ____/____/____

_____

_____

_____

_____

_____

_____

_____

_____

_____

_____

_____

_____

Sketches & Photos:

Description:

Date: ____/____/____

_____
_____
_____
_____
_____
_____
_____
_____
_____
_____
_____
_____

Place:
_____
_____

Time:
_____

Weather:
_____

Lunar Phase:
_____

Longitude:
_____

Latitude:
_____

Objects Sited:
_____
_____
_____

Equipment Used:
_____

Sky Placement:

Additional Notes:

Date: _____/_____/_____

Sketches & Photos:

Description:

Date: ____/____/____

Place:
_____
_____

Time:
_____

Weather:
_____

Lunar Phase:
_____

Longitude:
_____

Latitude:
_____

Objects Sited:
_____
_____
_____
_____

Equipment Used:
_____

Sky Placement:

Additional Notes:

Date: ____/____/____

_____

_____

_____

_____

_____

_____

_____

_____

_____

_____

_____

_____

Sketches & Photos:

Description:

Date: ___/___/___

Place:

Time:

Weather:

Lunar Phase:

Longitude:

Sky Placement:

Latitude:

Objects Sited:

Equipment Used:

Additional Notes:

_____

_____

_____

_____

_____

_____

_____

_____

_____

_____

_____

_____

_____

Sketches & Photos:

Description:

Date: ____/____/____

Place:

_____

_____

Time:

_____

Weather:

_____

Lunar Phase:

_____

Longitude:

_____

Sky Placement:

Latitude:

_____

Objects Sited:

_____

_____

_____

_____

Equipment Used:

_____

95

Additional Notes:

_____
_____
_____
_____
_____
_____
_____
_____
_____
_____
_____
_____
_____

Sketches & Photos:

Description:

Place:

_____

_____

Time:

_____

Weather:

_____

Lunar Phase:

_____

Longitude:

_____

Latitude:

_____

Objects Sited:

_____

_____

_____

Equipment Used:

_____

Sky Placement:

97

Additional Notes:

Date: ____/____/____

_____
_____
_____
_____
_____
_____
_____
_____
_____
_____
_____
_____

Sketches & Photos:

Description:

Date: ___/___/___

Place:

Time:

Weather:

Lunar Phase:

Longitude:

Latitude:

Objects Sited:

Sky Placement:

Equipment Used:

Additional Notes:

Date: ____/____/____

_____

_____

_____

_____

_____

_____

_____

_____

_____

_____

_____

_____

_____

Sketches & Photos:

Description:

Date: ____/____/____

Place:

_____

_____

Time:

_____

Weather:

_____

Lunar Phase:

_____

Longitude:

_____

Latitude:

_____

Objects Sited:

_____

_____

_____

_____

Equipment Used:

_____

Sky Placement:

Additional Notes:

_____

_____

_____

_____

_____

_____

_____

_____

_____

_____

_____

_____

Sketches & Photos:

Description:

Date: ___/___/___

Place:
_____
_____

Time:
_____

Weather:
_____

Lunar Phase:
_____

Longitude:
_____

Latitude:
_____

Objects Sited:
_____
_____
_____
_____

Equipment Used:
_____

Sky Placement:

Additional Notes:

_____
_____
_____
_____
_____
_____
_____
_____
_____
_____
_____
_____
_____

Sketches & Photos:

Description:

Date: ____/____/____

_____

_____

_____

_____

_____

_____

_____

_____

_____

_____

_____

_____

_____

Sky Placement:

Place:

_____

_____

Time:

_____

Weather:

_____

Lunar Phase:

_____

Longitude:

_____

Latitude:

_____

Objects Sited:

_____

_____

_____

Equipment Used:

_____

Additional Notes:

Date: ____/____/____

_____
_____
_____
_____
_____
_____
_____
_____
_____
_____
_____

Sketches & Photos:

Description:

Date: ____/____/____

_____

_____

_____

_____

_____

_____

_____

_____

_____

_____

_____

_____

Sky Placement:

Place:

_____

_____

Time:

_____

Weather:

_____

Lunar Phase:

_____

Longitude:

_____

Latitude:

_____

Objects Sited:

_____

_____

_____

Equipment Used:

_____

Additional Notes:

Date: _____/_____/_____

_____

_____

_____

_____

_____

_____

_____

_____

_____

_____

_____

Sketches & Photos:

Made in the USA
Middletown, DE
14 July 2019